Pancetta was not unlike her kitchen table: sturdy, yet fragile, delicate, wholesome, strong, pert, bouncy, and sensual. Despite the isolation of her farmhouse, when Pancetta saw the pickup truck drive up the dirt road, she was not alarmed. When she saw the strapping buck climb out of the driver's seat, she was not alarmed. When she noticed the bumper sticker saying, "Don't Come A-Knockin' If This Van Be Rockin'," okay—*then* she got a little alarmed.

ABOUT THE AUTHOR

Ronald Richard Roberts was born in 1930 in Boville, Idaho, where he has served as managing director of the annual pork festival for the past twenty-three years. He is also a Professor of Marketing at the University of Coeur d'Alene.

The Ditches is his first (and last) book .

RONALD RICHARD ROBERTS

THE DITCHES OF EDISON COUNTY

A SIGNET BOOK

SIGNET

Published by the Penguin Group
Penguin Books Ltd, 27 Wrights Lane, London W8 5TZ, England
Penguin Books USA Inc., 375 Hudson Street, New York, New York 10014, USA
Penguin Books Australia Ltd, Ringwood, Victoria, Australia
Penguin Books Canada Ltd, 10 Alcorn Avenue, Toronto, Ontario,
Canada M4V 3B2
Penguin Books (NZ) Ltd, 182–190 Wairau Road, Auckland 10, New Zealand

Penguin Books Ltd, Registered Offices: Harmondsworth, Middlesex, England

First published in the USA by Plume, an imprint of Dutton Signet, a division of
Penguin Books USA Inc. 1993
First published in Great Britain in Signet 1994
10 9 8 7 6 5 4 3 2 1

Printed in England by Clays Ltd, St Ives plc

For Perry Green

THE BEGINNING
OF THE END

Some melodies are borne of misty ponds around fields where unicorns roam, elves dance and there is no war . . .

Okay. I've been drinking. again. But at least I'm man enough to admit it. I'm all man, as a matter of fact. I've got a washboard abdomen, cast-iron pecs and a little friend that can make the ladies moan 'til the cows come home. And if you're willing to shlep to Idaho to find out, I can drink you under the table any day of the week, soldier.

Where was I? Oh, yeah. One day out of the blue

this guy and his sister call me from Florida. They tell me that they have a story they believe should be told, and I'm the only writer they know. (Little did they realize that I'm a folksinger, photographer and tuba player as well. I've also been a puppet, a pauper, a pirate, a poet, a pawn and a king. And I'm currently a marketing professor at a small midwestern university.)

So, they chew my ear about their story. It's more than a tale of romance, they say. It's an epic. It's this, it's that. It's a candy. It's a breath mint. It's two, two, two mints in one. Blah, blah, blah—thank God it was their dime.

The brother and sister wanted to meet with me personally to discuss it. A meeting sounded kind of formal, but I told them as long as the "conference room" had a liquor license and a pool table, they could count me in. I suggested Meat 'n' Eats on South Badger Avenue here in central Idaho.

At Meat 'n' Eats, the flawless preparation and service of fine food is a commitment. They offer an extensive children's menu and cater parties, too. Just take Highway 37 down past Old Post Road, and follow the signs. And I'd be remiss not to mention that I happen to be a proud shareholder in Meat 'n' Eats.

The brother, as I suspected, was an absolute windbag. But Sis was a bit of a looker, and, needless to say, she was eyeing me from the get-go.

Here is their story. It seems that a while back, their mother had this fling with a bohemian transient. For twenty years afterward she didn't tell anyone, but just couldn't live with the guilt. So when she kicked, the old lady left behind a letter to the kids, along with a box of photos, empty beer bottles and cigarette packs. There was documentation of every detail of each minute she spent with this two-bit Don Juan. If you ask me, it's a good thing the chick croaked before her brood discovered this collection. Had she not, I think it would have bought her a life sentence at the Ha-Ha Hotel.

The affair had took place in and around Edison County, Idaho, a town known throughout the west for the legendary ditches that pepper its roadsides. You haven't seen Idaho unless you've seen it from a ditch, and I've hidden, fallen, driven or passed out in damn near all of them.

I guess that's why they called me. If I hadn't taken that ad out in the Yellow Pages—or if they had actually read my work—there's no way they would have phoned. Because, see, my personal theory is, well, people will just basically disappoint you nine times out of ten. You heard me right—seventy-five percent of the time. Yup, half the folks you meet up with will just give you a raw deal.

"So?" I asked, polishing off a side of Meat 'n' Eats'

succulent, lime-smoked baby-back ribs—a steal at $6.95. "That's it?"

Maybe it was just a hunch, or maybe it was the booze—those Floridians could put it away themselves—but I thought I could write this sucker. Then again, maybe it was this brainstorm I had right around closing time:

"Look," I confessed, "I'm a lousy writer. And my photographs usually look like they've been taken through the bottom of a dirty ashtray.

"Your mama did have a damn good memory, though. I mean, her confession was obviously motivated by a certain amount of shame. And two drunken strangers doing the old slap-and-tickle ain't exactly *Wuthering Heights*. But this story has just enough of that New Age psychobabble to sell. We'll make the margins nice and wide, throw in some of the photos I could never unload anywhere else and charge an arm and a leg. I bet people won't even read the damn thing—they'll just buy it for each other on Valentine's Day. Let's get rich!"

By noon the next day, my first novel was finished.

WINTER 1992

CONCAVE, NOT COMPLEX

Ronald Concave prepared for his trip. Into the back of his van he threw the following: his cameras, a tire iron, several marionettes, a jar of Meat 'n' Eats Gourmet Recipe Steak Sauce, a worn copy of the self-help book How to Be Attractive to Bored Farm Wives, five golden rings, four calling birds, three French hens, two turtle doves and a partridge in a pear tree.

But his real baggage could never be thrown into the back of a motor vehicle. For Ronald Concave was a haunted man. A man with no friends. No family. No shirt, no shoes, no service.

If Ronald Concave's soul could have been examined by a doctor, it might have been diagnosed with halitosis, painful rectal itch, eczema, seborrhea and the heartbreak of psoriasis. Not literally, of course.

Because his mind tended to race with memories of yesterday, it was important for Concave to concentrate on the road ahead. He was traveling through a dimension not just of sight and sound but of mind. At the signpost up ahead, he noted LAST GAS—24 MILES. Last gas, indeed, thought Ronald Concave. Last gas, indeed.

He knew all too well what the sign meant. It meant that for the next 24 miles of his journey, there would be no service station. 126,720 feet. 1,520,640 inches. Luckily, the bladder of Ronald Concave was a strong, vital and robust one.

Days later, having driven across Texas, up through Oklahoma, and down across Mississippi and Kentucky, Concave consulted his map on the front seat. Unfortunately, because it had been upside down, Concave was struck with the realization that he had been going the wrong direction. "West," he told himself, "Idaho is west." ·

Getting himself on track, he drove back the way

he came, then followed the highway toward the Colorado River.

Concave began to think about his ex-wife, Miriam, the disagreements they would have. "Why don't you get a job?" she would ask. "What the hell is wrong with you, you lazy bum?" "I'm miserable and want to kill myself every waking moment that I'm around you!" And yet, despite Miriam's even temperament, Concave always sensed that something was a little off.

Often it was the little issues that led them into trouble—values, philosophy of life, whether or not to have children. But more often, Miriam and Concave fought about the bigger questions. Who gets the last beer. How many games should they bowl. And the one they went around and around with almost every night of their marriage—potatoes or stuffing?

In Comatose, Michigan, Concave pulled over and followed signs that read GIRLS GIRLS GIRLS—TRIPLE XXX-RATED MOVIES IN ROOM!!! He favored these inexpensive, out-of-the-way lodges for their hospitality and service. Passed out drunk that night on a stained bedspread that reeked of industrial disinfectant, he slept the sleep of angels.

The next day, Ronald Concave was back behind the wheel of his van, which he affectionately called Van. Through pastures, coal mines, fjords, flea markets and marine bases he motored. Past farmhouses and old steel mills. He drove through a little league field, after which a stern-looking attorney handed Concave his card and said, "We'll be contacting you shortly."

During his drive, Concave couldn't stop himself from humming the song Miriam and he considered theirs—"Teenage Lobotomy" by the Ramones.

At the Fickberg National Swamp, Concave was so overwhelmed by the area's natural beauty that he pulled over and ate lunch amid the algae and toxic waste.

"Ronald," an old lover once told him, "there is something inside you. It is hard to define, and harder to reach. But this thing permeates your being and scratches at your soul. I feel that you have been on this earth before, and after you die you'll come back again. In the meantime, don't take any wooden nickels, never eat at a place called Mom's and beware of people with two first names. Sorry, your time is up. That will be ten dollars." On second thought, maybe it was a geriatric fortune teller, and not an old lover.

Concave drove on, thinking about words. Certain ones thoroughly moved him. He loved the word "Kosher." "Snafu" was also a favorite. An utterance of the term "midwifery" could bring him to his knees.

"Juggernaut" and "flautist" caused him to weep openly, and "septic" he thought could be quite evocative.

He liked to make lists of these words, as well as phrases he believed should be spoken often:

Elvis has left the building.
Close cover before striking.
Don't sleep in the subways, darling.
For a good time, call Brenda.   555-6738.
Nam ham yo, ren-ge kyo.
Doo-wah-diddy, diddy-dum diddy-doo.

Sometimes he would think of locations with names he found enticing: Bora Bora, Fort Dix, Kummonaywannalaya, Big Sur.

Ronald Concave had always had an active mind. He just rarely used it. In high school, he started the Philosophy Club. There, he would share his dreams and observations about life, and the magic he believed he would someday find.

"Leprechauns exist," Concave would tell his classmates. "So do unicorns, gnomes, elves, trolls and fairies. They are among us. They are *in* us." Then he'd usually be hammered senseless by anyone near. Concave would often require the services of the legally blind school nurse, Mrs. Flavin, who was especially fond of administering stiches.

After high school Concave joined the Peace Corps, where he thought he and his special outlook on life would be safe. For two years he brought food and clothing to Marin County, California, unaware that it had an unusually high per capita income. Finally the town obtained a restraining order against him, and he again felt that he was misunderstood.

Such incidents failed to make Ronald Concave a bitter man, though. For one thing, he had his cameras. He could always take a picture of something, but for many years he preferred the majesty of a simple, black image. It represented, for him, a certain darkness in the soul of mankind. And he kept forgetting to take off the lens cap.

No one had ever complimented Concave on his photos, or expressed any interest in ever seeing them again, let alone publishing them. Yet something deep within him said that he must continue. Art was not necessarily something that people had to experience, validate or acknowledge in any way. And Art did happen to be the first name of a man who once sang with Paul Simon, whose song "Kodachrome" Concave greatly admired.

In the song's haunting lyrics, Ronald Concave saw himself—a man who owned a camera, and enjoyed taking a photograph. He often wondered if the song was actually about something else entirely, but this was the meaning that he, personally, extracted from the words.

After the Peace Corps, Concave moved to Pamplona, Spain. It was there that he had the accident. Going out to get his morning newspaper, he was trampled by an irate bull. He had forgotten that it was the day of the annual Running of the Bulls, which—ironically—was the lead story in that edition of the paper.

When Concave recovered from the massive head wounds a bull-trampling will cause, he moved back to the States. But jobs were few and far between for a man both as sensitive and as dense as Ronald Concave. He subsequently decided that he was wasting his life, and opted to live each day as though it were his last. Concave enthusiastically took up backgammon and hacky-sack. He even found the courage to begin watching prime-time television.

Now he crossed the Idaho state line. FAMOUS FOR POTATOES, the sign said. Hmm, thought Concave. Learn something new every day.

Concave turned off Route 71 and into the parking lot of a restaurant, Meat 'n' Eats. He had never seen such an impressive building, and the people inside looked as though they were enjoying delicious, savory food at reasonable prices. The sign outside the door informed him that the hours were EVERY DAY,

NOON TO MIDNIGHT, there was a smoking section and video game area for the kids, and all major credit cards were accepted.

Inside, Concave asked the manager about an attraction in nearby Edison County—a series of eight ditches alongside a road. Ditches of different shapes and sizes. The manager obliged Concave with directions, also pointing out that the blue plate special, chicken-fried steak, came with a double order of fries for just $4.95. "Now *that's* a deal," Concave exclaimed. "If I lived around here, I'd have every lunch and dinner at Meat 'n' Eats! And if I ever did anything interesting and got famous and wrote a book, I think anyone who read that book should go to Idaho and eat there many, many times!"

Concave called himself the Final Spaceman. He felt the word "astronaut" was too confining. A spaceman was what he dreamed of being as a kid, and now, thanks to several incidents involving massive blows to the head, a spaceman he was.

The world had changed, and he wondered if there was a place left for a man like him. But then, he had never before been to Edison County.

Concave found the first seven ditches easily. But the eighth ditch—called Sonnuva Ditch—eluded him. For a hole in the ground, you're pretty smart, Concave thought.

Driving around aimlessly, he spotted a mailbox that read *Dick Jackson.* Concave was no stranger to mail, and knew that if there was a mailbox on a rural route, chances were that a dwelling would be nearby. As he turned the corner, he saw that it was, in fact, the case.

Pulling Van up the drive, Concave saw someone on the front stoop. Someone dark and exotic, with long black hair, hoop earrings and a bandanna around the neck. "Excuse me," he said to the gardener. "You speak-a English?"

The gardener shrugged, just as an extraordinarily beautiful woman and her dog came out the door. The woman walked gracefully toward Concave. She had a delicate smile, lovely, tapered fingers and piercing brown eyes.

Good Lord, thought Ronald Concave with all of the longing in his heart. That is one sensational piece of ass.

PANCETTA

She was not unlike her kitchen table: sturdy, yet fragile, delicate, wholesome, strong, pert, bouncy and sensual.

The table's woodgrain sang out memories of days gone by. Metaphorically, of course—because in Pancetta's world, especially, there were no singing tables. Except for that fateful week, when even furniture could warble happy melodies.

She looked at a photograph of herself. In the many years since her affair with Ronald Concave, she had hardly aged, and the photo was proof: Her eyes were a deep blue. Her hair now matched them.

As she swayed, the woman in the photograph swayed. When she flicked a mosquito off her cheek, so did the subject of the portrait. Pancetta laughed to herself. How foolish she could be sometimes. She was looking in the mirror again.

It had been nine years since Dick had bought the farm. Kicked the bucket. Eaten lead. Whatever you want to call it, he was gone now. Decomposing. Pushing up daisies. Feeding the worms. Yup, there was no denying it—Dick was dead and stinkin'.

Pancetta was thrilled that neither of her children, who were now grown, ever called her. She had a special ritual that she felt they would not understand. Then again, they still had trouble understanding the alphabet.

Every morning, Pancetta would awaken in a cold sweat, which she followed with a hot bath containing homeopathic oils, exotic fragrances and chicken bouillon. While bathing she would cry incessantly, and after toweling off, she would beat her head against the wall. All for having let Ronald Concave enter her life.

Her name meant "bacon"—Italian bacon to be exact—and she had been named accurately. There was a rugged, smoky flavor to Pancetta's character, she was a good breakfast companion and she was not entirely bereft of grease. The nitrates part didn't quite make sense, however.

Pancetta was born in Bologna, or "Baloney," as the Americans prefer to call it. For a few years after high school she chased a dream called Happiness. But in Bologna, the only way to be content was to make your living stomping grapes with your feet, and she found that idea repulsive and more than a little nauseating.

She met Dick when he dodged the draft. She had never before served as a cover or provided a false identity for such a brave, strong man. When she came back to the United States, a priest married Pancetta and Dick. Later, they found out this was illegal, so they cut the priest out of the arrangement.

On their honeymoon—a budget affair at Mt. St. Helens—Dick and Pancetta made a conscious decision to realize their dreams. They chose to move as far away from civilization as possible, and do back-breaking, meaningless farm work for low pay. Dick was deeply enamored of the television show "Green Acres," and Pancetta was not about to break the news to him that it was a comedy.

Pancetta now faced an antique desk. She opened a drawer and removed one of two cans of Billy Beer. She had saved them for years. She also extracted a box that contained rare issues of *Reader's Digest*, a cork, a zipper, a pair of handcuffs, and a t-shirt that read MY PARENTS VISITED THE SONNUVA DITCH AND ALL I GOT WAS THIS LOUSY T-SHIRT.

As she sipped the lukewarm, rancid swill, Pancetta read a letter written on stationery printed with RONALD CONCAVE, TEACHER—WRITER—PHOTOGRAPHER—MUSICIAN—PAINTER—C.P.A.—MINI-BLINDS INSTALLATION.

June 10, 1985

Dearest Pancetta,

Hi! How are you? I am fine. I just took another writing class and I truly believe my work is far more better. But enough about me—let's talk about my photos. Enclosed are a few of you near the Sonnuva Ditch. You'll notice you're actually visible in a couple.

I still can't believe we did the nasty. I mean, what were we thinking?

Now I'm confused, Pancetta. You have changed my life in a wonderful, intense and important way. I'm miserable. And no woman has ever made me miserable before. Everything I see reminds me of you. A pigeon in flight. A field of alfalfa. A sneaker on the side of a highway. A rotten potato. A rerun of "The Jeffersons." See what I mean? I'm going mental here.

We must see each other again, Pancetta. And yet when I think of the actual prospect of doing so, I'd be less nauseous eating week-old sushi.

It's your move, toots.

Love,
Ronald

P.S. I had that little "problem" checked out. It seems that it's very common among men my age, it will correct itself and—I hate to say "I told you so"—but the doctor said the pliers were not a good idea.

Despite the isolation of her farmhouse, when Pancetta saw the van drive up the dirt road, she was not alarmed. When she saw the strapping buck jump out of the driver's seat, she was not alarmed. When she noticed the bumper sticker that read DON'T COME A-KNOCKIN' IF THIS VAN BE ROCKIN', then she got a little alarmed.

Pancetta had been raised not to make snap judgments, she reminded herself as the sweat-drenched Concave approached, blowing his nose on his t-shirt. Her dog, Yak, barked, but she calmed him with a blow to the head.

As Concave walked toward her, she couldn't help but notice that his legs alternated—left, right, left, right. It was as though he was letting them take turns. She could tell by this that Ronald Concave was a fair and generous man. Indeed, if his legs were children, neither would have felt neglected or abused when he walked.

He was as long and lean as a fat-free pepperoni. For a man of sixty-five, Concave was in remarkable shape. Unfortunately, he was fifty-five.

Pancetta wore a peasant dress by Yves St. Laurent, with a cotton v-neck t-shirt by Ralph Lauren, and soft suede sandals from Capezio. Her accessories were by Tiffany, and she pulled it all together with a smashing gingham Calvin Klein scarf. Her perfume, as always, was Unstable by Prince Manicotti.

At the fence in front of her house, Pancetta Jackson stood face to face with Ronald Concave.

"Excuse me," he said. "I'm looking for a ditch."

Pancetta turned away, the sun beating on her mane like Gene Krupa on speed. "Aren't we all," she asked rhetorically, "aren't we all?"

"No, really," explained Concave, "I heard there was a big ditch around here."

"Oh, a *ditch*," Pancetta said, "I thought you said you were looking for a *dish*. You see, I collect old dishes and silverware. I'm something of a maven—I can just never get enough place settings."

Concave was enthralled. He couldn't remember ever having cared much about kitchen accessories, yet suddenly he was obsessed with examining the knives, forks and spoons of a strange, sad and lonely woman.

"Well, if it's not too forward of me, I'd love to scrutinize your cutlery sometime."

"Why not join me for dinner?" she queried. "I guarantee you'll enjoy having my delicate instruments handle your meat."

"That a euphemism?" Concave asked with a smile.

"No," Pancetta said, bending to stroke the dog. "Half dachshund, half Saint Bernard."

———

Pancetta offered to show him Sonnuva Ditch. She hopped into Concave's vehicle as he made the proper introductions.

"Pancetta, Van—Van, Pancetta," he said, turning the motor over. As they pulled away, Yak barked from the front yard.

"I think my dog has a little crush on your wheels," Pancetta said, blushing.

She was taken aback by the condition of the

van's interior, which was packed with empty liquor bottles.

"Are these all yours?" she asked. "Did you drink all this stuff?"

"Oh, no . . ." Concave answered. "I—uh—I don't know where they came from. I've—actually—uh— never seen them before."

There was something about Ronald Concave that made Pancetta instantly trust him, instantly feel attracted to him and instantly reach for the seat belt, strap it across herself and pray that the vehicle was equipped with an air bag.

"So what brings you to Edison County?" Pancetta asked. "And don't say this van."

Concave laughed. "I like a lady with a sense of humor," he said, shifting gears. "Let me know when you get one."

Again, she asked him why he was in her neck of the woods.

"It's hard to explain," Concave said. "I look through a camera's viewfinder and select images to expose onto frames of film. I then have these works developed and printed on light-sensitive paper."

"Oh, so you're a photographer," Pancetta offered cautiously.

"Yeah, yeah. That's the word," Concave countered. "It was on the tip of my tongue." There was a sensual illiteracy about him, and Pancetta found herself momentarily wishing that *she* was the word "photographer."

"So you're photographing the ditches," she said. "Can I ask if you're on assignment?"

"Sure," Concave retorted. "Be my guest."

Touché, Pancetta thought. Now it was *her* turn to laugh at *his* lame attempt at humor. Then she realized he wasn't kidding.

"Well—are you?"

"I'm a freelancer, Pancetta," said Concave, remarkably guessing her name. "I walk my own way. I don't punch the clock or dance for the man. I like to have control over my work. When I'm finished, I plan to submit the photos to *Reader's Digest*."

Pancetta wondered if Ronald Concave knew that *Reader's Digest* was not the best venue for a photo essay. But something in his blue eyes told her that this spaceman had known his share of disappointment, and she was damned if she would be the bearer of even more bad news.

The trick now was not to disappoint or encourage him, but to deftly change the subject.

"Well, good luck with that," Pancetta said. "Hey—how 'bout them Dodgers?"

Concave drove on, repeatedly asking if he was getting close to Sonnuva Ditch. But Pancetta hadn't been there in years, and rarely gave anyone directions, so she was a little rusty.

"Okay, you're getting warm ... I think—no, colder, colder ... warmer, warmer—yeah, I think we're getting there ... no, colder ..."

"Are you sure you know where this ditch is?" Concave asked.

"Well, let's put it this way—I'll know it when I see it," Pancetta confessed.

If Ronald Concave were an angry man, he might have felt it in this type of situation. He had studied illustrations of Sonnuva Ditch in geography books. He had heard it described in stories told by his grandfather, and great-grandfather. And now, someone who lived within a mile of the ditch could not find it. This stupid, ignorant woman was wasting his bloody time on a sweltering hot day in a godforsaken town in the middle of nowhere. Luckily, Ronald Concave was a man not given to angry thoughts.

Then, just as he considered coldcocking her, Pancetta pointed ahead excitedly.

"Watch that possum, cretin!" she screamed. "Oh, by the way, here's the ditch."

They got out of the van. Then Concave ran it

down and shut the engine off. Damn—he always forgot to do that first.

The Sonnuva Ditch was splendid in its mundanity—five feet deep, perhaps twenty yards wide. Muddy water sat at its bottom, dry dirt lined the sides. Some local hooligans had thrown a few soda cans and empty snack-food bags into it, which in the hazy afternoon light added that much more character.

"It's going to be a challenge photographing this sucker," Concave said softly. "For one thing, this ugly covered bridge is going to get in the way. Damn! They're all over this county. It's either going to be in the background, or it will be in the way when I'm trying to get the proper angle."

"Why would anyone build a bridge here?" asked Pancetta. "Seems like such a waste of resources."

"Pancetta," he said, "there's an old proverb: 'Sometimes fools erect bridges when there is absolutely no need to.'"

"Really—is there really such a proverb?"

"Well, maybe not," Concave muttered, "but there sure as hell should be."

Pancetta couldn't help but notice Concave's body as he squatted near the ditch. It was different from her husband's. If Dick had tried to squat like that, he would have needed help getting up. It made her laugh inside.

"Pancetta," Concave beckoned. "Help me up, would you?"

They walked through a nearby field, ruminating spiritually as a hawk ripped the guts out of a barn swallow.

"How did you get your name?" asked Concave.

"Well," Pancetta explained, "when I was born, the hospital required a name for my birth certificate. The nurse, or whoever was taking down the information, asked my father. Luckily, he and my mother had prepared by selecting one."

"No, I mean, why 'Pancetta'?"

"Oh," she said and shrugged. "Who knows? Guess they liked overly salted, chemically processed meat by-products."

Concave was touched by her vulnerability. "When I was over by that ditch, I got something for you." He reached for her hand and placed something in it.

"It's—a handful of dirt," Pancetta said through her tears. "I—I—"

"I know you're moved, Pancetta," Concave intoned. "You've probably never gotten what you deserved out of life, and here a handsome, hard-bodied stranger is presenting you with a gift."

"I—I—I—".

"Don't try to speak. I don't blame you for being

speechless any more than I would blame Marcel Marceau. Don't try to describe this magic moment with empty words."

Pancetta sneezed. "Actually, I was going to say that dirt makes me really allergic."

They rode back to the house in silence, save for Pancetta's incessant, phlegm-producing hacking. Upon their arrival, Pancetta ran inside and returned with two glasses of amber liquid. "Iced tea?" she asked, handing Concave one of them.

Concave took the glass appreciatively and sipped the sweetened, caffeineated drink.

"Why, yes," he said, "yes, it is."

After he downed the beverage, Pancetta invited Concave into the house.

"How about a Quickie?" she asked with a wink.

Concave had never been a bartender, but he knew full well what she meant: A shot of rum, a jigger of lime juice, coconut milk and a sprig of mint. A Quickie. Delicious over ice.

He checked his watch. "Well, I was planning to go find a cheap motel, troll the bar, get depressed, then go back up to my room and pass out," he said. "But I could probably squeeze in having the drink, too."

Inside, Concave marveled at the simplicity and elegance of the decor in Pancetta's house. What simplicity and elegance, he thought to himself.

"So where is your family?" Concave asked.

"They're at the annual Pork Fair in Stockville," she explained. "Eating, sleeping and breathing pork for five fun-filled days and nights."

As they sat at the kitchen table, Concave pulled out a Camel and then offered the pack to Pancetta. "Animal Crackers!" she exclaimed. "I used to love these things."

"Do me a favor," Concave said. "Don't eat the Camels."

"Why?"

"They've always been my favorite. I guess you could say I've got a monkey on my back."

"For Camels?"

"Right."

"I'm confused. Can I eat your monkey?"

"I thought you'd never ask."

Concave cracked a six-pack of beer. Pancetta asked him a question that had been bugging her as long as she had known him—twenty minutes.

"So what exactly is the deal with you, mister?"

"Well, it's like this," Concave began. "When I'm not snapping pictures, I like to hike. I enjoy the gurgling of a mountain stream, and I am an award-winning fisherman. I write poetry and read six books a week. My favorite sport is tennis—I'm in a regular game every other Tuesday, and I also play eighteen holes of golf on Sundays. I'm a certified minister and perform between seventy-five and a hundred wedding ceremonies a year. I'm also a licensed locksmith and a notary public. Plus, I do tons of charity work."

"What do you do in your spare time?" asked Pancetta.

"Oh, I watch television quite a bit. That Weather Channel is 'something else,' as the young people would say."

Pancetta had a thought. And, as if that wasn't unusual enough, she was able to communicate it verbally.

"So what about dinner?"

"It's a great meal," Concave said with a smile. "As a boy, I remember eating dinner almost every night. Yes . . . the day would start out with breakfast. Then toward afternoon we would get hungry again, and often have lunch. By the end of the day, well, it was dinner time, all right."

"I mean, are you interested in staying for dinner?" Pancetta offered. "There isn't too much food here, but there is a chateaubriand for two which we could enjoy with a bottle of vintage Beaujolais, baby carrots in butter and asparagus with hollandaise sauce. I also make a mean crème brûlée—but if you want that I need to get it going right now."

"Sounds okay," Concave mumbled. "Except for the vegetables. I hate eating stuff that grows in dirt."

"But you can wash it off—"

She knew this would be a losing battle just from looking at his face. The veggies were simply a no-can-do. In fact, Pancetta feared that Concave was thinking about having his dinner instead at Meat 'n' Eats, Edison County's finest nightspot, freeway close and with plenty of convenient parking in the rear.

"I wrote something down in my journal last week," Concave said. "It was a dream I had. Shecky Greene was borrowing money from me."

"The comedian?" Pancetta asked.

"Right. He needed forty dollars to get his Harley fixed. He was going on an odyssey to find himself. We were in Tahoe, though, and I was afraid he was going to gamble the money away. So he said, 'Fine, putz. I'll just ask Siegfried and Roy.' I remember feeling quite hurt and betrayed."

"You are a strange, mysterious and intriguing man, Ronald Concave," said Pancetta Jackson.

"And what the hell is that supposed to mean?" replied an irate Ronald Concave. "God, my mother used to tell me crap like that."

Concave got up to go check on Van. On his way out, he slammed the screen door, breaking it into several small pieces which now lay in a pile on the ground.

Pancetta took a bath. She felt that there was something cleansing about using soap and water to get all of the dirt and sweat off of her body. She pretended the soap dish was a lantern, and that she could rub it to have a wish come true. She wished Concave would walk in on her accidentally and make passionate love to her. If not, her second choice was that he didn't loot her house and drive away. Pancetta's third choice was that tonight's "Hawaii Five-O" episode wasn't a rerun.

As she dried herself off, she looked out the window to the front yard. Concave was flossing Yak's teeth. Though the dog seemed uncomfortable and tried to get away, Concave persisted in demonstrating patience and concern for the animal's oral hygiene.

When she came downstairs, Concave was at the kitchen table, on the phone.

"Speak up—I can't hear you," he said, unaware that Pancetta stood behind him. "Oh, Bombay's always hot this time of year. Yeah . . . drink a lot of water. And stay away from the open air markets—lots of pickpockets . . ."

As Concave paced, he noticed Pancetta.

"I gotta go," he said, hanging up quickly and turning to her. "Just—talking—um—to a friend . . ."

"In Bombay?" she said, with obvious irritation. "That's a toll call. Do I look like Jackie Onassis here?"

"No, it's Bombay, uh, Idaho," Concave stammered. "Don't tell me you've never been there. Oh, man, it is the neatest place. I mean, you talk about a great little town ... hey—how would you like a beer?"

"Cold and quick," replied Pancetta, not unlike the beverage in question. Concave spit out the cap he had taken off a frosty one and handed it to her, raising his own.

"To ditches, good friends, good food and Lowenbrau," he said. "Gosh, I love that commercial."

As Pancetta turned her back to him and started on dinner, Concave looked at her. He had never seen a rump like hers. And this spaceman had seen his share of rumps. Pancetta's posterior was as well-defined as the word "statutory" in a law textbook. He thought once or twice about tackling her by her thin ankles and having his way with her. But something told him the night called for slightly more romance than that particular gesture would afford.

"Can I help with the work?" he asked, praying that her answer would be to shake her head "no" and hand him the remote control.

"Well, you could slop the pigs, if you don't mind," answered Pancetta as she tenderized the steak with a croquet mallet. "Then you could mow the lawn, wash the car, go to the post office for me and start folding the laundry."

"Oh, I don't know," Concave said, sitting back down. "My back's kind of been out . . . I think I ruptured my, uh, compact disc."

"Sounds pretty bad."

Pancetta turned on the radio and found a country station. Billy Bob Nimbus was singing his hit, "Psychic Breakdown." "I'm thinkin' of a number between one man and ten . . . ," he sang, "I got a ugly premonition she's cheatin' again . . ."

"I saw a large case in your van. What's in there?" Pancetta asked inquiringly.

"Oh, that's Brian," said Concave, jawing open another brew.

"A child? Oh, my God. I'll call 911." Pancetta ran for the phone.

"Chill, Pancetta," Concave said, smiling. "Brian is my tuba."

Pancetta was relieved, and impressed. "You play the tuba?"

"Yes. It was all I got in the divorce. I sing, too. I accompany myself on Brian. I know all of Sousa's oeuvre, as well as a few songs I wrote myself. You see, someday I hope to write a bestselling book and release an album of songs that exploit its success."

Concave noticed that Pancetta had started to cry. He was certain that the idea of him belting out a love song on a large brass wind instrument had saddened her.

"Are you okay?" he queried.

"Can you cut these onions?" she asked. "They're doing quite a number on my sinuses."

"Sure," Concave said as he began dicing with gusto. "By the way, if it's not too forward of me, I'd love to spray an antihistamine up your nasal cavity."

"Let's get to know each other a little better," Pancetta demurred. "Maybe in half an hour."

Pancetta took the meat and sliced it in half with her cleaver.

"So, your divorce . . . what was that like?"

There was silence. Pancetta sensed that Concave didn't want to discuss his disappointing marriage.

"Well?" she asked again.

"Huh?" Concave said.

"I asked what your divorce was like."

"Oh—I thought that was the radio. You know, one of those call-in shows. . . . Let's see, what was my divorce like? It was like a separation, only more permanent."

"What made it seem so final?" Pancetta asked.

"Well, it might have been the note she left, which said, 'You are the most disgusting, horrid human being I have ever met. I never, ever want to see you again. Good-bye, loser.' That, and the fact that she took almost everything I owned and sent her brother over to beat the molasses out of me a week later."

"My goodness," Pancetta marveled. "What happened between you two to cause this?"

"I beat her at Scrabble," Concave said sheepishly. " 'Dermatology.' Eleven-letter word, fifty-point bonus, the whole shebang."

Pancetta knew what this must have felt like. She remembered taking Dick to the cleaners in canasta one night, and there was hell to pay.

"Ever hear from her anymore?" Pancetta wondered.

"She's a professional wrestler now. Goes by the name 'Hacksaw Hannah.' "

Pancetta was starting to feel the alcohol. Nine beers usually didn't present such a problem, but tonight, maybe she *wanted* to be drunk. Snookered. Loopy. Dizzy. Pickled.

As she often did for no apparent reason when she was drunk, she started saying the word "blubber" over and over. "Blubber . . . blub-ber . . . blub-ber . . ."

Concave arched an eyebrow. Cupid's arrow hits at the oddest times. "You know, Pancetta Jackson, you are about one Frito shy of a bag, but I think I love—"

He stopped himself. "I think I like—I think I can tolerate you."

"I think I can tolerate you, too, Ronald Concave—at least for dinner," Pancetta said, then winked, looking down as Yak hugged her guest's leg. "And the dog seems pretty taken with you, too."

"Sweet mother of mercy!" Concave screamed. But he had to smile—it was the most physical affection he'd gotten in years.

When Yak was finished, Concave smoked a cigarette as Pancetta continued to prepare their meal.

"It sounds malodorous in here," he ruminated, and Pancetta chose to just let the comment go by like so much cross-town traffic. She had the feeling that the drunken Concave was about to pontificate pretentiously, and wondered if she—a farmer's wife—would be able to understand him.

"I'll tell you a little something about art," he began. "It's all a game. The young punks get all the glory. They go to all the hoity-toity openings and drink designer water, and put pieces of crap on the wall and call it 'painting' or 'photography.' Then it sells for thousands of dollars, they get their kissers into *Vanity Fair*, and voila—a fraud is born."

"Oh," Pancetta offered.

"But I'm not bitter," Concave said, kicking the dog out the door. "I mean, it's a living."

AN UNWARRANTED INTERRUPTION FROM RONALD RICHARD ROBERTS

Hey—it's me again.

So is this a great story or what? I mean, it's got everything—ditches, sex-starved dogs, dreams involving Shecky Greene ... I gotta say I'm feeling good about this. I mean, this little book could really sell. I could pay off my credit cards. I could finally see Majorca. And I don't even want to.

Between you and me, though, I'm praying that something happens, story-wise, pretty soon. Don't get me wrong—while conducting my research I became pretty taken with Pancetta and Concave, in a twisted sort of way. But things *are* kind of slowing down.

So, I'm starting to panic a little. I mean, they say you really need to keep things moving in a novel. But then they also say you shouldn't go into the water in less than thirty minutes after you eat. And they say love is blind.

Who exactly is "they" anyway? My friend Larry thinks it's actor Hal Linden. You know, the guy who played Barney Miller.

OUT TO
PASTURE

Pancetta burned the steak, so she scrapped the menu in favor of an old standby: boiled quail, ham hocks and Velveeta, and cold prune soup. It was good, hearty, stick-to-your-stomach food, and Concave ate it with the energy of a male vocalist contestant on "Star Search."

"So," Concave said as he licked his plate clean. "What next?"

"Well, I'm certainly not about to play you in Scrabble," Pancetta said, laughing.

"How about a little racquetball?"

"Sounds a little strenuous," said Pancetta. "Let's take a walk instead."

"Fine," agreed Concave, as he limped toward the front door. "But let's leave the dog here, if that's okay."

Concave loved the kind of night he and Pancetta were strolling through—muggy but windy, the skies threatening.

"The Native Americans call this 'Muggy but Windy Night of the Threatening Sky,'" he bluffed.

"Yes, I know," said Pancetta.

Concave pulled out one of his cameras and asked Pancetta if she would mind being shot.

"Who wouldn't?" she said. "I mean, what did I ever do to deserve—"

"With the camera, bimbo," he countered affectionately. "I like to shoot—er, *photograph*—at night, because my pictures tend to come out a little dark, anyway."

"Whatever," shrugged Pancetta.

"Okay," Concave prompted as she posed and he started clicking off shots. "Some more teeth, baby—yeah, that's it—I love it—uh-huh . . . yeah—you are one *hot* fox—yeah . . . bend over a little, pretend that flower is a—yeah, oh, that's beautiful, honey—what a sexy, sexy thang . . ."

"Ronald . . ." Pancetta said through her smile.

"Show me the magic, sweet meat . . . shake your

bootie and do your special little number ... you're the best, cupcake—you're a star—"

"Ronald!"

"What?!?"

"Did you put film in the camera?"

"Oops."

Consolingly, Pancetta took his hand, and they continued to walk. "Shhh ... that's a whippoorwill ... shhh."

"A whippoorwill goes 'Shhhh'? That's a whippoorwill?" Concave said skeptically. "No way. A whippoorwill goes like this: 'Coo-ah-coo-ah-coo—'"

"No, I said 'shhh' because I thought I *heard* a whippoorwill, moron. God! You take everything so literally!"

"And what is *that* supposed to mean?" Concave asked defensively.

"It means I just don't know how this is going to work, Ronald. Maybe we should break up."

Concave was devastated. There was so much they hadn't done. They hadn't had a child. They hadn't bungee-jumped. They hadn't been to a bar mitzvah. They hadn't eaten dessert. He sat on a rock, looked at the moon and tried the old poetry gambit.

"I meant what I said/I said what I meant/An elephant's faithful/One hundred percent ...".

Pancetta rested her head against his clavicle. "Why, that's Dr. Seuss . . . *Yertle the Turtle?*"

"*Horton Hatches the Egg,*" Concave corrected her.

"Ah, yes," she said, although she had not actually been able to make it all the way through the book.

"Seuss had it all," Concave went on. "Economy of language. Stylistic brilliance. Large, funny-looking mammals of questionable origin."

"I eat my peas with honey/I've done it all my life/It may seem kind of funny/But it keeps them on the knife," Pancetta recited.

"Nipsey Russell?" Concave asked.

"Ogden Nash." It was liberating for her to swap cultural passions with someone. Edison County was not exactly full of big brainers. Stooges, buffoons and dunderheads aplenty, but not much Mensa material. Most of these idiots hadn't even *heard* of Seuss, Nash or Russell.

The two circled back to the house. "Say, would you like some fruitcake?" Pancetta said.

" 'Would you like some fruitcake?' There—I said it," countered Concave. "Hey, this is fun. Can I give you something to repeat now?"

Pancetta fixed a stare on him. "Ronald," she said. "I have invited you back into my home. You now have two choices. You can either get into that smelly old death trap and drive aimlessly, looking for a place to

sleep and probably ending up passed out amidst the
filth and vermin of your back seat, or you can spend
a few more hours flirting romantically with a sexy, nu-
bile younger woman ..."

"And that would be ..."

"Me, Numbnuts!"

Concave scratched his head. "Can I think about
this? I have trouble making quick decisions."

"All right, but Dick is coming back in a week."

"Thanks, but it's a decision I have to make alone,
Pancetta. There's no reason to believe that your husband would want me to spend the night with you. I
mean, we *know* what he would say. He's biased."

Pancetta walked through where the screen door
had once been. "I'll be inside," she muttered, "slicing
the fruitcake."

Concave thought to himself. If only those damn
bridges weren't there, he could have gotten the shots
he needed of the ditches, and he would have been out
of Edison County. But now he found himself being
drawn back to Pancetta's sweet breath and ample
bosom. Mostly the bosom, he had to admit. Both bo-
soms, actually.

"Wait up, toots," Concave purred. "Don't get all
bent out of shape—I'm coming back in."

Pancetta searched high and low for an appropri-
ate after-dinner beverage. In the back of the refriger-

ator she found two bottles. " 'Yoo-Hoo Chocolate Energy Drink,' " she read on the label. "Hmmm."

"Hey, it's got Yogi Berra's picture on it, it must be good," Concave said, settling back into his chair at the kitchen table, which was about as comfortable as Rush Limbaugh at a NOW rally.

Concave was about to do the open-the-bottle-with-his-teeth schtick again, but Pancetta held on to the vessels. "C'mon," she cooed. "Save those lip muscles for something important."

"You're right," said Concave. "That fruitcake looks like it'll be mighty chewy."

As Pancetta poured the Yoo-Hoo, he wondered how many times her slim fingers had prepared sweet, low-fat, high-protein dessert drinks for misguided, unfocused, mentally challenged wanderers. Just once, he hoped. Including this time.

"To walking in pastures on moonlit nights and successfully avoiding animal droppings," he toasted.

"To walking in pastures on moonlit nights and successfully avoiding animal droppings," she said smiling, clinking her glass with his.

Oh, thought Concave, real original.

Concave drained his Yoo-Hoo and inhaled his piece of fruitcake. Pancetta moved close to him.

"Well," said Concave. "I hate to eat, walk, quote poetry, take pictures, eat again and run, but I have to be at the Sonnuva Ditch by noon. And this hangover's gonna be about as cooperative as a caveman at an electrolysis session."

Pancetta was severely disappointed, but didn't want to seem desperate.

"Don't you want to stay and—and have another piece of fruitcake? Or—use the bathroom? I've got some great magazines in there. My stamp collection is extensive—we could look at that . . . or—do you play bumper pool? There's a table in the basement. Or there's always TV—there's a special two-hour 'Columbo' on, and I could make Rice Krispy Treats . . ."

"Hold on to that fruitcake," said Ronald Concave as he turned to walk out the door. "That creep you married might not share it with you, but I guarantee that you will finish it with someone special. And we will always think about tonight. Maybe not today, maybe not tomorrow, but forever, and the rest of our lives."

"*Casablanca?*"

"Actually, I thought it was from *Valley of the Dolls.*"

"No, I'm pretty sure it was *Casablanca*," Pancetta said as she started doing the dishes. "Not the part about the fruitcake, of course—the other stuff."

"Quit stalling, Pancetta. I'm outta here. Call your dog off my van so I can get on my way."

And with that, a rather ornery, intoxicated and

disoriented Ronald Concave started up his van and drove off, taking into his shaky hands the lives of anyone who dared walk the streets of Edison County, Idaho.

Back inside, Pancetta took out a Post-It Note and scribbled a message on it. She then got in her car and sped off toward the Sonnuva Ditch.

On her way, a van coming from the opposite direction clipped her and almost ripped off the driver's side mirror.

"Stupid schmuck!" she screamed, not bothering to notice who the driver was.

HE SHOOTS ...

There was something familiar about the farmhouse Ronald Concave passed on his way out to the Sonnuva Ditch the next morning. He couldn't tell what that something was, though.

Inside, splayed out on her bed like freeway roadkill, lay Pancetta Jackson. She had a man-size headache, and the man's name was Ronald Concave.

Ronald Concave. Twenty-four hours ago, it was probably just a name on a photo in a U.S. Post Office. Or maybe several. Now it was part of her life.

She let the name roll off of her lips. Then she gargled repeatedly.

And then Pancetta heard Van—the unmistakable sound of a motor vehicle in desperate need of repair. As it chugged toward the Sonnuva Ditch, Pancetta's heart began to stir.

"A fluff-muffled Truffle will ride on a Huffle/And, next in the line, a fine Flummox will shuffle," she rhapsodized, thinking again of thoughts Seuss.

Concave barely made it to the ditch, and unloaded his supplies for the shoot. He had stalked this prize and now would make sure it was his.

He took out his light meter. Read the light. Set up his tripod. Attached the camera. Read the light again. Adjusted the tripod. Screamed. Fished the tripod and camera out of the ditch and started over again. If ever there was a consummate professional, Ronald Concave could have used him on this photo shoot.

Finally, Concave was ready to take a picture. Tilting the camera down into the mouth of the ditch, he saw nothing. Then he took the lens cap off. Looking through the viewfinder, he again saw nothing. Then he focused.

What he saw in the ditch astounded him. It was a note tacked to the west wall. At the top, in block letters, it read RONALD CONCAVE. That immediately

told him the note was for him. For the Final Spaceman had just that kind of smarts.

Ronald removed the note, and put it and the
thumbtack in his back pocket before continuing to
shoot. After another couple of photos, he was ex-
hausted, so he loaded up Van and took the driver's
seat.

But he had forgotten about the thumbtack.

Concave's scream echoed through the canyons
and ditches of Edison County, all the way to a farmhouse on the other end of town, where Pancetta Jackson smiled knowingly.

Back in the van, Concave pulled out the note
and read it through teary eyes. "All ready to put up
the tents for my circus. I think I will call it the Circus
McGurkus." Seuss.

Within seconds, Concave had stopped at Meat
'n' Eats to use the pay phone. A lunch crowd had developed, and were enjoying the various bountiful
offerings on the menu—hamburgers, barbecued
chicken, fried shrimp. Concave couldn't help but notice how happy the children were, while the adults—
many of whom were tourists who had come to see the
ditches—were clearly thrilled by the value.

Concave found several listings for "Jackson,
Dick" in the Edison County phone directory. One was
a hairdresser who had studied with Vidal Sassoon and

enjoyed reading mysteries. Another was a gas station attendant who had once served seven years at Lompoc for illegally transporting fertilizer across state lines. Yet another was a night watchman at the local K-Mart who claimed that he had regular visitations from the ghost of William Frawley, television's beloved Fred Mertz. Four were brothers, working their way through school because their no-good father left them years ago and their mother was laid up, never having quite recovered from her hip-replacement surgery. Concave promised to keep in touch with all the wrong numbers he got, as he thought it the proper thing to do.

===

Pancetta happened to be at home, pacing her kitchen floor, trying to remember the words to the song "Louie, Louie" when the phone rang.

"Hello?"

"Pancetta?"

It was Dick. She could tell because she had been married to him for several years, and had grown accustomed to the sound of his voice. Pancetta had such acute intuitive skills.

"Why, hello, Dick," said Pancetta, trying to sound normal.

"Everything okay?" he asked.

"Sure, yeah, everything's okay—why do you ask?"

"Because I care about you. Because we've been married for fifteen years, had two children, and created a life together."

"Oh."

"So—nothing's new?"

"Well, I haven't had dinner and gotten drunk and eaten fruitcake and taken walks with any really handsome, older, transient writer/photographers, if that's what you're asking," Pancetta said as her Call Waiting beeped in. "Oh, that's another call. Hold on."

Pressing the button on the cradle, Pancetta purred, anticipating the caller.

"Hello, my love," she cooed.

"Pancetta, what the hell is wrong with you?" asked Dick. "It's the mid-seventies. Call Waiting hasn't been invented yet. I've got a good mind to come back early from this trip. You on drugs or something?"

The drug wasn't one she could tell her husband about. In fact, little did Pancetta know that as she hung up on her husband, the drug was getting through on the telephone line.

When the phone rang again, she picked it up and shouted, "Listen, pal. I don't give you crap about your little three-day excursions to go buy a new pig out in Des Moines, do I? Nor did I question the pack of matches I discovered in your trousers last year with the name Florinda and a Wichita area code written on the inside! So don't start giving me an earful about—"

"Pancetta. It's Ronald."

"Oh. Sorry. Come on over."

"Listen, I can't. I've still got to shoot the Fallinda Ditch at four. But if you'd like, you can watch me work. I guarantee my back muscles will ripple at least a little. And let's face it, it beats hanging laundry or manicuring the sheep or whatever the hell you do all day."

His respect for her was overwhelming. "I'm there, Spaceman."

Concave waited for the light to fade by going into town and seeing if he could stay out of fistfights. This proved unsuccessful, as his DAYTONA BEACH SPRING BREAK—I WAS THERE!!! t-shirt drew stares from several of the locals.

"Hey, lookie there—I reckon that-there long-haired feller is a stranger to these-here parts," said one of them, a tractor mechanic.

"Indeed, he hath little regard for the ways of this village," retorted his friend, a noted Shakespearean scholar.

Later, Pancetta met up with Concave and he seduced her in the rituals of photography.

"You want to really jam that film in there, plunge

that shutter release and keep cocking that frame advance," he said, and she felt herself melting.

She watched Ronald Concave squat, kneel and hug Mother Earth, all in pursuit of the perfect photograph of a hole in the ground. And it simply made Pancetta Jackson excited, she had to admit.

"Whoo-boy!" Concave said, smelling his armpits. "Either something crawled in there and died, or I need a shower."

Pancetta wanted nothing more than for him to use her bathroom. But she knew that the only way to handle Concave was to play hard-to-get.

"How would you like to shower at my place?" she asked. "I've got a nice, big loofa that would just love your pulsating muscles."

"Why, that's a nice gesture. I'd be happy to rub your loofa all over my tanned, firm, blood-engorged, hard-to-believe-it's-middle-aged body."

Pancetta thought Concave had a healthy self-image—and that he was an egomaniac.

Concave followed her home. Inside, he showered. From downstairs, she could hear him singing "I Will Survive." He did a serviceable Gloria Gaynor impression.

This kicked off a medley of Neil Sedaka, K.C. and the Sunshine Band and the Pointer Sisters. It was a long shower.

Pancetta, meanwhile, prepared dinner. She had earlier been to a package store and requested a pound of spaghetti and a bottle of knock-out, hundred-proof whiskey, praying that old Mr. Fenster wouldn't sense anything wrong. But he asked her what it was for.

"Well, it's not because I'm trying to bed down a rugged, drop-dead gorgeous freelance writer/ photographer, if that's what you're wondering."

Fenster shrugged and shook his head. "I mean the spaghetti," he clarified. "You making some of that marinara sauce of yours?"

After she had gotten the ingredients for dinner, Pancetta went to buy some new clothes. Concave now came downstairs, drying off his hair, and saw her in them for the first time:

"Hooooooo! Whoa, baby—hhhhhuuuuuhhhhh . . . Ya-ya-ya!"

"You like?" asked Pancetta.

"Like what?" Concave answered. "This towel must have had a—arrrgggh!—a furball or something on it. I'm—I'm chok—choking!"

And with that, Pancetta Jackson stood behind Ronald Concave and applied the Heimlich Manuever. Squeezing her delicate left hand into a ball, she gripped it with the slender fingers of her right, jammed it under his perfectly articulated rib cage, and thrust upward.

Frightened, Concave stomped the floor like a baby, and Pancetta soothed him.

"Easy, there . . . easy . . . *hey, douche bag—do you want to live or die?!?*"

Whatever it was finally dislodged, and he turned to stand face-to-face with her. It was at that moment that Pancetta Jackson sincerely wondered what this man was doing in her house.

... HE SCORES

When the telephone rang, Pancetta froze.
Concave reached for it, but she knew that
wasn't the way to handle the call.

"Hello," Pancetta said.

"Pick up the phone before you start
speaking," advised Concave.

"I was practicing."

Pancetta took a deep breath and lifted the receiver.

"Hello," she began. "Oh, hi, Peg. Yeah, everything's okay. I'll tell you one thing—there have
been no mysterious strangers around this way hav-

ing dinner and taking long walks with me—heh, heh . . ."

Pancetta listened for a while, and then looked at Concave, rolled her eyes and made that "yak-yak-yak" sign with her hand.

"Listen, Peg—I've got to go . . . I'm, uh, making a . . . chestnut soufflé, and I've got to check on it . . . talk to you soon—bye-bye."

She hung up the phone.

"You didn't tell me we were having chestnut soufflé," Concave said, licking his lips.

"We're not," Pancetta answered. "I just needed to make something up to get off of the phone. And chestnut soufflé requires constant attention. It's not just the folding of the egg whites and the grating of the chestnuts, but the oven temperature has to be monitored every six to eight minutes. Then it has to sit for a half an hour to cool.

"Peg said there was some demented-looking stranger in town today," Pancetta went on. "Apparently several of the men came to blows with him, and they wanted to make sure I hadn't seen him. They say he appears dangerous."

"I'm scared," Concave admitted. "What if he comes here tonight?"

"Ronald, get a grip. Demented-looking? 'Dangerous'? They're talking about you."

He opened two beer bottles. Pancetta had never seen such dexterous teeth. As he set them dramatically on the table, Concave saw her legs peek out of her skirt. He knew that something very powerful was happening between them. Not between her legs, but between him and Pancetta Jackson.

She turned the radio on. The song playing was Captain and Tennille's "Muskrat Love."

Ronald Concave was a hopeless romantic. Immediately, he thought of the episode of "Batman" in which Batman dances with Jill St. John. With the savoir faire of a young Adam West, he leapt to his feet and grabbed Pancetta's arm.

"Let's get funky," he whispered.

They danced. Pancetta put her head on his shoulder, and he breathed in the aroma of her perfume. It smelled like Napalm in the morning. It smelled like . . . victory.

Pancetta felt awkward. Stifled. Confined. "Ronald," she said. "Get off of my foot."

After the dance, they sat out on the porch. Pancetta asked Concave about his philosophy of life. This "Final Spaceman" stuff. And why he thought the Mets had such a lousy infield.

"There are certain things that distinguish us from gorillas," Concave began what was certain to be a pompous, amorphic and utterly incoherent speech.

"One very obvious example is our desire to go bowling, often on a weekly basis. Bowling is an activity that presents human potential in an awesome way, Pancetta. The whole notion of trying to knock ten pins over with a heavy orb is mystical, if not primal. And if you can't knock all of them down—or even one pin down—there is a second chance. The almighty spare.

"We wear special shoes for this ritual, Pancetta. Because a bowling alley is a refuge, a place of worship, a character-building institution. We wipe our hands on towels and resin bags, and we keep them dry because we are doing important spiritual work.

"There wasn't always bowling. We created bowling. And maybe there won't always be bowling, but I sure do hope there is.

"Maybe we'll destroy it, though, like we did with most everything else that was great—James Dean, corner drugstores, those little souvenirs you buy on vacation with the snow in them, that you shake, the metric system, candy pants . . ."

He chugged down his beer and continued.

"I'm the Final Spaceman. I am an unfriendly alien on a friendly planet, a planet that says you have to have a job, bathe and shower often, and have a pleasant personality. But why, Pancetta? Why?

"The Greek philosopher Testicles once said: 'The

worth of a man's life is easily measured. It's simply desire, plus passion, times the square root of anger, divided by the truth.' He was really more of a mathematician than a philosopher—and I was never very good at math—but I think there's something to it.

"Interesting story I once heard. Seems an old man was napping against a haystack on his farm. Bunch of teenagers came by and asked him for a dollar.

" 'If I give you a dollar,' the old man said, 'you will then think that money need not be earned.'

"So they ask him for his cow.

" 'If I give you my cow, then you will think that material possessions are easily obtained.'

"They didn't have to ask him another question. In fact, they looted his house, found his shotgun, stole his car and riddled the old man with bullets as they left. It's an important story, more for what it doesn't say than for what it says . . ."

Concave had been watching the stars when he heard the commode flush from inside. Pancetta came out of the house.

"I—didn't see you leave," Concave said.

"Where were we?" sighed a refreshed Pancetta. "Oh, yes. You were going to tell me your philosophy of life." She moved closer to him. "But if you just want to hump, that would work, too."

Concave felt himself falling into Pancetta as she groped him. "Unless you're too drunk, that is."

"Who you calling drunk, Mrs. Cameron?"

" 'Mrs. Cameron'?" asked a shocked Pancetta.

"*You're* the drunk—*you're* the stinkin' drunk!" Concave shouted. "I mean, where do you get off giving me a C minus in English? Where do you get off? You pretentious little Ivy League snob—I could strangle you!"

Oddly, Pancetta was enchanted. She knew this was just Ronald Concave's unique method of foreplay—that he was a special animal who communicated at a different pitch than mere humans. She felt her pulse jump and her adrenalin race. Despite the fact that she was dragging him upstairs by his hair, there was an undeniable aggressiveness about Concave.

"Uhhh ... uhhh ..." he said, dominating her as she took his shoes off, unzipped his trousers and unbuttoned his shirt. "I think I might have to puke," Concave whispered in her ear, and once again she was electrified by a sensation which could only be found in the films of Russ Meyer and the songs of Barry White.

"I'm excited too, Ronald," Pancetta said between gasps as heavy as sweet cream.

"No, really—I'm in bad shape here, baby . . . how about a little breathing room?"

"You're making me crazy, Ronald Concave," Pancetta declared to her soulmate. They then proceeded to make love for five blissful, uninterrupted minutes. For Pancetta, it felt like ten. For Concave, an eternity.

Afterward he lit a cigarette. But a casual toss of the match into a wicker trash basket ignited both it and the bedroom curtains. Concave fell back asleep while Pancetta tried getting the fire out.

"Ronald!" she screamed. "Wake up! If my husband returns and half the house has burned down, he'll know something was up!"

"Okay, honey—I'll take out the garbage," Concave murmured, rolling onto his stomach.

"I love you, Ronald Concave," Pancetta Jackson sighed as she swiped at the flames. "And I want you to take pictures of me so that I can stare obsessively at them for the rest of my life. Not right now, of course. Right now I think you should get some sleep."

"Yes, mother."

"And eventually it might be a good idea to stop drinking, Ronald. But that's just a suggestion."

ANOTHER TOTALLY UNNECESSARY NOTE FROM THE AUTHOR

So. They did it.

Thank God. I mean, how much time can two people spend making idle chit-chat? I know for me, personally, if I'm not getting somewhere with a lady after a couple of hours, I start looking at my watch a lot. I mean, I wasn't put on this earth to analyze last night's dream or read your astrological charts, honey. So let's either put the pedal to the metal, or call it a day. Que será, and all that.

So, just as I would feel if I were in Concave's

shoes, I _am_ feeling a little confined now. I mean, if I were him, I'd be out of that bedroom like a jackrabbit on pure-grade Colombian nose candy. But that would entail certain qualities that the "Other Ronald" doesn't seem to possess. Like common sense. Survival skills. Or, for that matter, consciousness.

Maybe it's just as well. I mean, my word count is currently about as low as his brain-cell count. So perhaps a few more verbal volleys, some more extraneous sex and a meaningless philosophical exchange or two are _exactly_ what is needed.

Yeah. These two should get to know each other a little better. Absolutely. After all, that's what life's about.

THE FREEWAY
AND THE PIGEON

R onald Concave took a few days off from his work, which qualified as his greatest contribution to the art world to date.

He and Pancetta spent virtually every waking hour in each other's company—laughing, making love, fishing, eating waffles and smoking clove cigarettes.

Pancetta drove with Concave to the Big City, where Concave needed to have his glasses cleaned. Pancetta had never been to the city, and marveled at the world her lover was introducing her to—a world of parking meters and two-story buildings.

On the way back to Edison County, Concave took Pancetta out to dinner at a very special restaurant—Meat 'n' Eats.

Pancetta opened up with a salad, drenched in blue cheese dressing, then moved on to the pan-fried catfish and a baked potato with all the fixings.

For Concave, it was shrimp cocktail, and a twelve-ounce filet mignon with peppercorn-sherry sauce.

The two shared a hot fudge sundae for dessert, and each of them had coffee. Total tab: $27.85.

"So reasonable," Pancetta noted. "And so good!"

After returning to the house and going at it like wild animals, Pancetta and Concave knew it was time to have a very important conversation.

"Ronald. There's something on my mind."

"That's a switch. How do you suppose something like that happened?"

"I mean, we need to have a talk—it will affect the rest of our lives," said Pancetta. "What are we going to do with each other?"

"I sort of have this plan," Concave confided. "Your husband comes home. I'm waiting behind the front door with this big rock, see, and when he comes in I smash in his skull. Then we drag his body to a nearby small business and torch it to the ground, making sure not to leave his eyeglasses behind—that is, if he wears eyeglasses—"

"Ronald," Pancetta said, shaking him. "That's been done. It's *Body Heat*—it's *Double Indemnity.*"

"Never saw either one."

"Really?" an impressed Pancetta noted. "You've got a good imagination. You should think about writing."

"Ah, who's got the time?"

Pancetta tried to recapture her original train of thought.

"Ronald, I like the skull-crushing thing, but it sounds messy. What about confronting Dick? What about just telling him flat-out that you've never met anyone as wise, beautiful and wonderful as me, and you love me more than life itself, and that you want to take me away and spend the rest of your life with me?"

"In other words, lie."

Pancetta began to cry.

"I'm kidding," Concave said, applying a series of well-deserved noogies to her pate. "You're so sensitive."

"You said something last night when we were playing Hide the Salami," Pancetta recalled through her tears, "something about you being the father, the son and the holy ghost, the Three Stooges and the Seven Dwarfs all rolled into one. That our love is forever, like a biker's tattoo on your soul. That you wanted to take me to baseball games, to the circus, to a Robert Goulet dinner theater production of *Fiddler on the Roof*. You talked about our beings merging—if not into one, then into two, or five, or at the very most nine."

"I was really drunk, Pancetta. I wish you'd stop riding me."

"Don't you love me, Ronald?"

"I love you like a flower bed loves peat moss. Like Shields loves Yarnell. Like a river loves the rain. Like Norman Mailer loves himself. Like—like—"

"I feel the same about you, Ronald. You are old socks to me. You are the good kind of cholesterol. You are rayon. You are that stuff you find in the corners of your eyes when you first wake up in the morning. You are the stars, the moon and several small unidentified cloud formations. You are at once a Japanese warrior and a diaper rash. You are tuna salad that has been in the sun a little too long—"

"Let me take you away from this life, Pancetta," Ronald implored.

Pancetta loved him when he implored. But she was resistant.

"Ronald," she began (for that was his name), "I

have a family. I have a husband who despises me and takes me for granted, and two children who think the world owes them a living.

"Them I could leave behind. But not the dog, Ronald. Not Yak. He is everything to me. He is the sunset of a lazy afternoon. He is a beacon of light over a darkened field. He is salty pretzels. He is hard-boiled eggs. He is—"

"Okay, okay, I get the idea. Jesus, it's a mutt, Pancetta!"

Pancetta looked deeply into Concave's ice-blue eyes. "If you take me with you, it would be okay with me, Ronald. If you decided to settle down, in some small town on the east coast—Sacramento, or Butte, or Chattanooga—that would be fine."

"Those towns aren't on the east coast, Pancetta," Concave pointed out.

"I was a poor geography student. I don't know how I ever got that degree in Comparative Literature from Columbia, with a minor in World Religion.

"Anyway, I don't think us spending the rest of our lives together is a good idea," she continued. "I mean, I'm just not sure that we have that much in common. I'm a woman, you're a man. I live the lonely, pathetic existence of a farmer's wife, you live the lonely, pathetic existence of a delusional bohemian. I like to cook, you like to take pictures of holes in the ground . . ."

They held each other. And held each other. For three days, in fact, they held each other. Pancetta held Yak. Yak held Ronald.

Then Ronald whispered to Pancetta, "I've got to tell you something, and I'm only going to say it once. I'll say it once, and that will be it. Yes sir, that's just gonna be it. One time only."

"Okay, already," said Pancetta. "Get on with it."

"Well, there comes a time in a man's life when he just realizes what's done is done. What's up is up, what's down is down. The universe is irrational. When the moon hits your eye like a big pizza pie, that's amore."

The next day, he was packing to leave. The Final Spaceman was getting ready to take off, to launch himself into a dusty nether world called Tomorrow.

Ronald made sure that this was a moment his soul mate would remember forever—a bittersweet, heart-tugging parting of the ways between star-crossed lovers.

"I gotta split, babe," he muttered.

Pancetta nodded. "Later, dude."

"See ya."

Through moist eyes she watched him swat Yak off of the top of Van and start the vehicle.

"Don't go!" Pancetta screamed.

"What?" asked Concave.

"Stay—stay here with me. We can make this work . . ."

"But what about your husband, and your kids? And don't you have a bridge game—"

"You're right. Go. My mistake—you're right. Definitely go."

"Pancetta, you're wearing me out," Concave said. "Can I write to you?"

"Write me, call me. You can even send digitally reproduced graphics to me over the telephone line—if they ever invent it."

"You mean 'faxing'? Oh, that's still ten or fifteen years away. Now, I really need to go, Pancetta. I mean, enough is enough, girl."

Pancetta nodded sadly as Van screeched away.

Concave turned on the radio, and didn't look back until she was almost out of view. When he saw her, she was beating the dog senseless.

———

Dick Jackson and the kids returned to an immaculate house with a full meal on the kitchen table.

"Dad," said Calamine, his daughter. "This ain't our house."

She was right. In fact, when they entered their

own house, it was a pig sty. Pancetta brushed off her dress as she greeted them.

"So—how was the Pork Festival?" she asked innocently.

"Really boring, Mom," said Calamine.

"It sucked. What's for dinner?" asked their son, Migraine, in his idiosyncratic way.

Only Dick seemed revitalized and energetic. He pulled a wrapped gift from his pants pocket and handed it to Pancetta with a smile.

"Pork jerky!" she exclaimed, trying to feign interest.

"Honey smoked," said Dick. "Paid a pretty penny for it, too."

After the children retreated to their rooms, Dick pinned Pancetta against the refrigerator.

"How's about a little hubba-hubba, sweets? It's been almost a week."

"Oh—I—have to fold the laundry," Pancetta stammered. "But—um—maybe in like a month or two . . ."

Luckily, Dick was oblivious to virtually anything Pancetta said to him.

"Any interesting mail come in while I was gone?"

"Male? A male? As in, 'a male human being'? Named Ronald Concave? Who showed me love in a new and exciting way? Who opened spiritual doors I had never before known of? No, no, there has been no such male. Why? Why would you ask?"

"Pancetta, I think you better lie down or something," said Dick. "You're goin' completely batty."

She knew that Concave would be in Edison County for another three days, and hoped that Dick didn't need to go into town anytime during that period.

"Where's all the beer and food?" Dick asked, looking in the refrigerator. "Let's go into town."

"Town? What do we need to go into town for? We're self-sufficient here, aren't we? We can—grow the things for dinner, and—and—brew beer if we need to! Let's get ambitious, here! We can create everything we need right here without going into town!"

"Get in the goddamn truck, Pancetta," Dick said, grabbing his keys.

In town, Pancetta kept her eye peeled for Van. At a gas station, she saw it—and so did Dick.

"Look at that beat-up jalopy," Dick laughed. "Whoever's driving that thing must have his head up his butt. I mean, what kind of jerk would try to get around in that wreck?!"

Pancetta watched as Concave lovingly pumped ethyl into Van.

"Maybe he's an adventurous, hard-bodied freelance writer/photographer who treasures emotional growth and self-empowerment over material gain."

Dick eyed Pancetta suspiciously.

"Just a guess," she said sheepishly. Pancetta considered getting out of the truck right then and there and declaring her love for Concave—in front of old Zeke, who ran the filling station, his wife, Irene, and young Walter, who liked to dress up like Liberace and scare the local children.

But her judgment got the best of her, and instead Pancetta began muttering to herself the mantra that kept her sane in such trying times: "If it looks like a duck and walks like a duck, it's a duck. If it looks like a duck, and walks like a duck, it's a duck."

It didn't work in this case, though, and Pancetta broke out in tears. Au revoir, Ronald Concave, she thought, confident that Dick would not hear her. Her sobbing continued, though, unabated.

"Pancetta! What in tarnation is wrong with you, woman?" asked Dick.

"Oh, uh—I think, I think I have a little eye infection. I, um, accidentally poked it with a dinner fork last night. Or maybe it was the night before. I've just got to be more careful with my silverware, no question about it."

Dick could only shake his head. There were times when his little lady could be quite a boob.

DUST NEVER
SWEEPS

Despair. Loneliness. Misery. Another night in
Edison County.

It was Pancetta's seventieth birthday, and
lying on her bed, she could see the headlights
of a van. She could hear its barely operational
motor.

Getting out of bed, Pancetta realized why
these things were happening. The gardener was there,
just like every other Wednesday.

Nonetheless, she continued to carry a torch for
Ronald Concave. When she slid her hand over her

stomach, she felt his hard abdomen. When she brushed her hair, she felt his tender touch. Often, she considered seeing a specialist.

Thank goodness that Pancetta had her kitchen table. It was the same table that Concave had eaten off of and passed out on. It was really less of a table than a shrine for Pancetta—a living testament to a love she once knew. Well, maybe not living, but standing. So to speak. Because it had legs.

Pancetta enjoyed polishing the table, wiping the table, having conversations with the table. The table never talked back, of course, but that was just fine with her. It was loyal, unwavering and dependable. Unlike the chairs, which would often tip over and have to be reprimanded.

She never contacted Ronald Concave, but a package arrived in the mail a few years back. It contained an issue of *Reader's Digest.* The magazine contained no article, photos or mention of Ronald Concave, but she knew what it represented. It was the issue his photographs might have appeared in, had the magazine actually published photography. The other condition, of course, would have been that Concave had any talent.

In addition to the magazine, Concave had sent an Animal Crackers box, the label from a bottle of Yoo-Hoo, and a photograph of himself. In the picture, he was smiling, vibrant, well-lit and happy. Pancetta could tell two things about the shot: that he was obviously far away from Edison County, and that Ronald Concave did not take the photograph himself.

She kept these items in a place she knew her husband would rarely look—her side of the bed. And thanks to Ronald Concave's periodic communication, she was able to glimpse, up close, the gradual deterioration of both his body and his mind.

One of the last packages she received contained a photo of Concave in a silver Spandex jumpsuit at a disco. Pancetta knew that these establishments were fashionable, but felt a tinge of jealousy that her former lover was boogying his nights away.

Then she noticed, in the photo, a gold filling in one of Ronald Concave's back teeth. Looking closer, she saw that the filling was inscribed. There were words, which, holding the photo extremely close to her face, Pancetta could actually read:

"Pancetta," the filling read, "light of my life, heart of my heart, the finest woman I have ever known, in all my born days, as I live and breathe."

After Dick expired (cause of death: eating way too fast), Pancetta thought about phoning Ronald Concave. Finally, she decided to give it a try.

It was a simple matter of going to the library—the closest one was seventy-five miles away—finding several listings for "Concave, Ronald" and then hiring a private investigator to follow up on them.

Pancetta nervously dialed the number she had been given as Concave's.

"Al's Laundry," the voice on the other end said.

"Ronald?" asked a hopeful Pancetta.

"No, this is Beverly. There's no Ronald here."

"I'm trying to reach Ronald Concave. He's about seventy-five, with a long, lean, hard body. About fifteen years ago he came to town and he and I—"

"Listen, lady," said Beverly. "You got the wrong number. Now are you gonna get off the phone, or do I have to call the fuzz?"

"It was a romance to last a lifetime," Pancetta continued. "You see, he was a photographer, and I was a bored, lonely farmer's wife. Well, one thing led to another, and the next thing you know—"

"Lady—please—I gotta get back to work."

"Okay," Pancetta relented. "By the way—do you guys dry clean sweaters?"

"Uh huh."

"Even the ones with little sequins? I can't seem to find a place that can do those delicately."

"Sure, bring it in—we'll take a look at it," Beverly said.

Pancetta put the receiver on the cradle with mixed feelings. No, she was probably not going to find Ronald Concave. But a good dry cleaner was nothing to sneeze at.

Pancetta called *Reader's Digest*. "We've been trying to get ahold of him for years," a woman named Ima Boar told her.

"Really? To publish his work?" Pancetta asked.

"No, he owes us six ninety-five for a subscription," the woman replied.

Another employee at the *Digest* remembered Concave well, however. "He was very diligent about approaching us," the man said, his voice shaking. "In fact, you might say *too* diligent. He stalked many of our editors and caused us to relocate our offices several times."

That was Ronald Concave, Pancetta thought. Mr. Never-Say-Die, Mr. Stalker, Mr. Disgruntled. Very few men had that kind of persistence and indefatigability. Very few women had it, either. Or children. She once knew an insurance agent who came close.

Two years ago another package arrived at her doorstep. The return address was a mortuary. Never a good sign. Her heart pounding like a Buster Douglas left hook against Mike Tyson's jaw, she opened the letter that was enclosed:

April 1, 1990

Mrs. Pancetta Jackson
Edison County
Idaho

Dear Mrs. Jackson:

Are you sitting down? Lover boy is vapor. That's right, he's dead as a doornail.

Pancetta knew what this meant. The odds of a rendezvous with Ronald Concave had just gotten significantly slimmer.

Apparently, according to the attorney's letter, Concave had taken part-time work as a mover, and a piano fell on top of him, killing him instantly. It was ironic that Ronald Concave's beloved music would ultimately do him in.

His estate is valued at forty-five dollars. He insisted on having these items sent to you, as you are the only person who ever loved, cared for or, for that matter, would even speak to Ronald Concave.

Also enclosed is a letter to you from Mr. Con-

> cave, in the envelope sealed with happy face stickers.
> If his writing is anything like his photography, we
> send out deepest regrets should you decide to read it.
>
> Sincerely,
> Howard Eino, Attorney at Law

Pancetta opened the box. Then the box inside that. And the next, smaller box. She then extracted the bag, out of which she drew the bubble-wrapped cotton, inside of which was a small jewel box, which contained a small piece of gold. It was the filling.

Also in the package was the note she had left in the Sonnuva Ditch.

It was all quite a bit for Pancetta to handle. And if that wasn't enough, there was the letter from Ronald Concave dated October 30, 1987:

> Dear Pancetta,
>
> I have little doubt that as you're reading this
> you will be a little bit stirred-up emotionally. You'll
> probably be a psychotic, nervous wreck. That was
> how I left you. In fact, that was why I left you,
> but at this point, me being dead and all, that's water
> under the ... ditch.
>
> I probably shouldn't be quite so flippant about

being six feet under, as they say, but it beats the holy heck out of being in that house with you, Pancetta.

Nonetheless, there have been a few occasions when I wanted to ring you up. One was when slam dancing came into fashion. I thought it was something we would have enjoyed together. Another was when the Mets won the Series in '86. I know you're not a big baseball fan, but did you happen to see that sixth game? It was something else.

I did phone you several times, but always under the guise of a prank or phony phone call. I was the one who asked if you had Prince Albert in a can ("Well, for God's sake, let him out"), and if your refrigerator was running ("It just ran around the corner"). I was also Mr. Hamburger, Piccolo Pete and Randy, the man from the Gas Company. I'm deeply sorry that I stooped to this level just to hear your voice, but hey, nobody's perfect.

So what have I been up to? Well, I finally did get notification that Life magazine wanted to use my work in a special issue devoted to me. It turned out to be an old grammar school chum playing a joke on me, but even that was an honor.

Seriously, the last few years have been very tough for me. My heart has had a hole in it. The doctors tried everything. I couldn't even go near a ditch without falling to my knees in pain. I think you created the heart problem, Pancetta. Leaving you was the stupidest thing I've ever done in my life, aside from a sexual incident involving hard drugs, an off-duty nurse, and a rubber hose, which I'd rather not get into.

I got myself a pig and named it Pancetta. Pretty weird, huh? But it was nice to utter your name to her on a regular basis, and the snorting she emitted was a great ice-breaker when we'd walk on the beach.

Seuss once wrote, "From a country called Frumm/Comes this Drum-Tummied Snumm."

I don't know exactly what that means, but I think it has something to do with man's inhumanity to man, the fate of the earth and the position of the cosmos. Either that, or he just thought the words sounded neat.

I love you, Pancetta. I honestly love you. It's a groovy kind of feeling. Like I said, though, I'm dead. So any feeling at all, at this point, is welcome.

The Final Spaceman,
Ronald Concave

P.S. By the way, I ran into Dick at Bingo Night last week, so I knew sending you this stuff wouldn't blow our cover.

He doesn't look bad for a dead guy.

Pancetta's last act in this bizarre celebration of dysfunctionality was to read Concave's self-proclaimed masterwork. Picking the camels and monkeys out of a box of Animal Crackers and opening a bottle of Yoo-Hoo, she read it.

TUMBLING INTO DEMENTIA

RONALD CONCAVE

There are nursery rhymes I still can't follow, cartoons that scare me and certain clothing fasteners I can't figure out. I have tumbled into Dementia, where the national language is double-talk, the favored sport is bungee-jumping, and all domestic animals are required to wear plaid pants.

In Dementia, a rose is a rose is a rose. But the men share a deep-seated desire to be Joey Heatherton, and several of the children pass the time by throwing lacrosse balls at each other's heads.

I am a primal beast in these territories, a savage who can barely walk erect, let alone play hockey with any proficiency. Yet I persevere. For I, too, quest an answer to a question once asked by the Russian philosopher Niblick: "If the meek shall inherit the earth, what will all the obnoxious, annoying people get?"

Dementia is a riddle, trapped in a sphinx, shrouded in a conundrum and wrapped in paper full of those little kids with the huge puppy dog eyes. It is a town called Hope, in a state called Misery, in a country called Despair. But there are some lovely condos downtown. One has French doors and a service porch, and five thousand could get you in if you can call me by two-thirty. I have two other couples interested, though, and I want to be fair to them—they have kids to think of.

We dance in this place called Dementia. We dance of life, and spirit, and out of a deep desire to issue a commemorative stamp featuring the cast of the TV show "F Troop." We also play softball wearing oven mitts, and every Wednesday is Prince Spaghetti Day.

A soft polka pulls me gently toward my love. Tonight, as I lift her, I have the strength of ten men: Moe, Larry, Curly, Grumpy, Dopey, Bashful, Sleepy, Happy, Sneezy and Grumpy. Did I already said Grumpy? Yeah. So who am I forgetting? Oh, yeah—Doc. I always forget Doc.

———————

When the fog lifted and the sun shined over Edison County, Pancetta Jackson took the contents of the package, and put them in her desk drawer. Then she laughed, because if she didn't laugh, she knew she was going to cry.

A LETTA
FROM
PANCETTA

Pancetta Jackson breathed her last breath on May 13, 1992. She died several weeks later.

She was seventy-three years old. Ronald Concave would have been well into his eighties. Zsa Zsa Gabor is forty-two. Jack Benny would have been thirty-nine. Macaulay Culkin is ten. And how about that Dick Clark—does he look great or what?

A few years before her death, Pancetta asked that when she died her body be thrown into the Sonnuva Ditch. Her children, Migraine and Calamine, found this rather odd, as it was their family custom to be frozen and stored under Disneyland.

After the ceremony, the children went through all of Pancetta's worldly possessions. For the most part, they were sorely disappointed—Migraine was rather amazed, though, by his mother's extensive collection of Tony Orlando collector's plates.

It was Calamine who found the documentation of Pancetta's roll in the hay with Ronald Concave.

"Migraine," she said. "Migraine—wake up."

"Huh?"

Calamine's voice began to quiver. "Mom had—a—little—you know, she—with a guy—and—both of them—together . . ."

"Oh my God," Migraine said as he made a startling realization. "She had a brother we never knew about?"

"No." Calamine shook her weepy head. "She—and this—guy—"

"Okay," Migraine said, calming her and taking her hands, "sound it out."

Calamine stood up and used the charades gestures familiar from her childhood.

"All right," Migraine said. " 'Mom,' right? Okay, 'Mom was' . . . *something* 'around.' Two syllables. Sounds like 'trucking.' Let's see . . . 'clucking' . . . 'ducking' . . . 'plucking'—oh, my God."

The kids were appalled. They couldn't believe the loser their old lady chose to have an affair with. "Quite a legacy," Migraine sighed as he read through Ronald Concave's prison rap sheet. "This guy's accomplishments make Dad seem successful."

Then they found an envelope which had *Migraine and Calamine* written across the front.

"It must be for us," Calamine said,

"I think you're right," observed her equally dim-witted brother.

Calamine read the letter to him.

"November 12, 1990

Dear Calamine and Migraine,

    Since I'm probably not going to be around forever, I thought I'd write this note and make a confession that shouldn't be put off any longer.

    Remember that tuna casserole I used to make for you? With the celery and olives and onions in it? Well, that recipe wasn't really mine. I got it out of a book.

    But that isn't what this letter is about. What it's about is, well, I never actually darned your socks. I had them sent out. There, I said it.

Okay, that wasn't it, either. What I want to share with you is that when you and your father went to the Pork Fair in 1974, I was not exactly doing what I said I was doing back home.

You may recall that when you returned I said I had a daily routine of not wanting to get out of bed, cleaning the house, moping, having lunch, contemplating suicide and doing the yard work.

The reality is that I met a man who rocked my world. His name was Ronald Concave.

This man was inept in so many areas I don't know where to start. He was an awful writer. As a photographer, he could be compared to Ansel Adams only in that both of them owned cameras.

He came to town that summer to take pictures of the ditches. His photos were so terrible that National Geographic took him off of their subscription list.

As a lover, Concave had the tenderness and sensitivity of Don Rickles. When he was conscious, that is. He liked to drink, and would become extremely boisterous and opinionated. He once insisted that egg salad was completely overrated as a lunch choice, and went on for hours justifying his position.

Ronald Concave was otherworldly. Which other world, I'm not sure. He was simple, yet complex. Elegant, yet casual. Robust, yet fruity, with a bouquet all his own. Perfect with beef or chicken.

When I first met him, he wanted directions to a hole in the ground. By the time we parted company there was a void in my soul much larger. I mean, you talk about a hole, this is the Grand friggin' Canyon, here.

Children tend to not think about their parents in sexual terms, but I have to tell you kids that Ronald Concave was one hunk-a hunk-a burnin' love. He was the wind beneath my wings. An Adonis. Rod McKuen meets Luke Perry. If they ever make a movie about him, I think Robert Redford would be perfect. Unless he demands gross points. Movies are just too expensive these days to give that much away above-the-line.

One night in the middle of making love, I whispered to Ronald that he was quite a beast in the sack. He replied, "I am the mighty Oz. I am the freeway, and the pigeons, and all the pizza crusts people have ever left on their plates. I am woman, hear me roar. I am curious, yellow. I am the eggman, you are the walrus, coo-coo-coo-choo. I am yours, you are mine, we are what we are. I am what I am, and that's all I am. I'm dreaming of a white Christmas, just like the ones I used to know. I shot the sheriff, but I did not shoot the deputy.

"I like Paris in the springtime. I like New York in June. I like Ike. I have always depended on the kindness of strangers. I can't believe it's not butter. I can't believe it's a girdle. I sing the body electric. I go to Rio."

Okay. He was a little self-obsessed.

I tried to contact Ronald Concave only once after he walked out of my life. This attempt was unsuccessful, but did yield an important relationship with a reasonably priced dry cleaning service. In fact, I still owe them $4.75 for a blanket, the receipt for which I have enclosed.

So, anyway, that's about it. I don't know why I'm telling you any of this. But I thought that if you were curious about who I really was, this might help to explain some things.

Stay away from fried food,
Mom

Migraine and Calamine were silent. He broke the silence.

"What a slut."

"Migraine, come on," said Calamine. "Don't you get what happened? She pined away for this loser for years and years! She would have been even more pathetic than she already was if she had stayed with him. This is actually great news!"

Before she had even finished, Migraine had gone to the toolshed and returned with an axe.

"Outta my way, Calamine," he ordered, swinging the axe over his head. "No *wonder* my life stinks!" he screamed, splitting the beloved kitchen table. "No *wonder* I make my living as a Peggy Lee impersonator! No *wonder* I spend half of my paycheck on a shrink!"

"Migraine!" Calamine shrieked. "Get a grip!"

He did not stop until Pancetta's beloved kitchen table was a pile of toothpicks.

"We're *so* dysfunctional!" Calamine sobbed.

"Is there any booze here?" asked Migraine. "I need to get plastered."

Calamine searched high and low and finally dug out a fermented bottle of Yoo-Hoo, which she poured into two glasses. Migraine toasted bitterly. "I hope this kills me."

Calamine, meanwhile, took out the notebooks of Pancetta Jackson, her mother, and began reading to herself.

"There's an old saying—'Beware of strangers driving old vans and working as freelance photographers.' Or, if there isn't, there should be . . ."

POST MORTEM:
THE WHIPPANY
DODO

I n writing about Ronald Concave and his extraordinary relationship with Pancetta Jackson, the need arose in me to find out more about the man.

    For one thing, it was important to learn where Concave had come from in order to understand where he was going, why he made the life choices he did and what experiences had prepared him for this unusual romance.

The main reason, though, to be totally honest, was that my publisher, Jake Weiner, was furious at me. I had promised a manuscript of a book, and given him, basically, an extended magazine article. He claimed there weren't enough pages to justify having it bound. In fact, he said that his wife had read the entire story while in the john, and, according to him, she wasn't even in there much longer than usual.

"Where's the story?" he asked me. "I mean, I've eaten pancakes thinner than this thing! Boy meets girl, boy shtups girl, boy leaves girl? That's a *story?!?* Give me a break!"

I knew then and there that the Pulitzer Prize was a longshot. But a breach of contract was all too possible, and according to Jake's lawyers I needed to pad this thing out considerably to deliver the book I was contracted for.

As a tax write-off, I flew to New Jersey, where Concave had spent many years, specifically in a town called Whippany.

After a week-long tour of the neighborhood watering holes, I was beginning to think I was on a wild goose chase. Then I bought a bourbon for a guy who turned out to be the former warden at a nearby correctional facility.

The warden hooked me up with a man named Sam "Dodo" Droppings, who shared a cell with Concave in the late 1950s. (A look at the police blotter told me that he had been convicted of dismemberment during a school talent show. Apparently, in addition to his other delusions, Concave fancied himself a professional magician. On this particular occasion he had attempted to saw a classmate in half without having researched the proper execution of the trick.)

Droppings was a musician by trade—a percussionist, to be exact. His instrument of choice was the cymbals, and in prison, Dodo often accompanied Concave when he played his tuba, Brian. As this was incredibly noisy, both Dodo and Concave were routinely flogged for this behavior by the staff and other prisoners.

I tracked down Droppings at his tiny apartment over a prosthetic limb shop in Whippany. It took some prodding and several quarts of hard liquor to get him to open up about Ronald Concave, but after a while I couldn't shut the guy's piehole. His long-windedness couldn't have been better for me, though—I knew I had finally found the ending for my book.

Please note: What follows is a transcript of my interview with Mr. Droppings, along with my notes, which have been made in editing.

INTERVIEW WITH SAM "DODO" DROPPINGS

Yeah, I knew Ronald Concave. Knew him well. Real well, as a matter of fact. That's what happens when you share a cell with someone.

In those days, of course, a hamburger cost twenty cents. A Coca Cola was a nickel. A head of lettuce, twelve cents. Or sometimes, nine, if it was starting to get brown around the edges. Milk? Well, that was ... [Approximately ten minutes' explanation follows about goods and services and their prices from several years ago.]

I was doing short time at Whippany Correctional

when they brung in old Ronald Concave. Actually, he wasn't that old at the time. He was a fair bit younger than me. There wasn't no hair on his chest. His body was firm, with taut, hard muscles. You could see the definition of his rib cage; he had a washboard abdomen. His legs were strong, like a soccer player's . . . [Four minutes on the hardness of Concave's young body.]

Never used to jam much. You know, the cymbals are an instrument very few cats can play well, and even fewer cats can play them solo. But when Concave took out that tuba and started wailin' away on her, I knew I had me a partner. He called the instrument— Brian, I think was the name—and he played that thing the way Willie Mays played center field. The way Oscar Robertson passed a basketball. The way Count Basie tickled the ivories. The way . . . [Three minutes on how well Concave played the tuba.]

We jammed together quite often. The song we really cooked on, man, was "Louie, Louie." That is one bad-ass tune for tuba and cymbals, brother, I'll tell you.

After a few months, they sprung Concave out of the joint. That's when he bought that van of his and started taking them, what do you call them— photographs. Boy, he took a liking to that camera of his. It became like his best friend. If he was Robinson

Crusoe, that camera was Friday. If he was Sherlock Holmes, that camera was Watson. If he was Juliet, the camera was Romeo. Although, it would probably make more sense that he was Romeo, and the camera [Four minutes on how much Concave loved his goddamn camera.]

Didn't hear much from Concave for several years. During that time, they actually let my sorry ass out of that jail. I started playing at a local club called Winky's. It was a nice enough club, but Winky, he didn't pay you much. Yes sir, Winky was pretty tight with the dollar. It was his belief that the performing exposure was valuable, and so, subsequently, there was very little financial compensation. Sometimes he acted like you should be payin' him . . . [Twenty-three minutes on what a cheap bastard this Winky character was.]

Concave never talked much about his life since being in the stir. Except for one night, when I seen a fillin' in the back of his mouth. We had been drinkin' pretty hard, and I was layin' there on the floor pretty close to him. So I saw this fillin', and lookin' directly at it I noticed that it had something carved into it, you know, inscribed-like. And what it said was, *Pancetta.*

"Pancetta?" I says to him. "You mean, like, Italian

bacon?" And he nods his head, real sad-like, and starts to tell me about this woman he met down Idaho way.

She was somethin', accordin' to Concave. And when he talked about her, his nose started runnin' and his eyes welled up with tears. He began talkin' about disappointment, and how some things last forever, but disappear before you know it, while other things last only a few days, but feel like they take a lifetime. [Six minutes on bizarre time-space continuums.]

I asked Ronald if he was takin' any medication, because, you know, he was startin' to talk a little nutsy. But the more he described his fling with this Pancetta woman, the more I realized that sometimes you don't need no drugs if you already ain't quite right in the head. And believe me, the more he talked about that week in potato country, the more I thought the little men in the white suits needed to pay him a visit.

Concave pulled out a box of them Animal Crackers as he went on. He was partial to the camels, as I recall. He picked up his axe case, removed Brian—his tuba—and started blowin'. I joined in on the cymbals, and by dawn we had written a tune called "Pancetta." Also, by dawn, several tenants in my building had moved out.

In the morning, we played the song again, and ate camels, and laughed, and cried. Then he grabbed his stomach and ran into the bathroom. In ten minutes he was dead. I knocked his fillin' outta his mouth before the cops got there, and the pawn shop gave me five dollars for it.

I got me a picture of that Sonnuva Ditch in my bedroom. Concave didn't take it, which of course explains why the ditch is visible. Once a month, or maybe once a year, I take out my cymbals, stare at that photo, and play that song we wrote, called "Pancetta."

On second thought, maybe it's not quite that often. You want to grab somethin' to eat? I got me a big hunger. They opened a new rib place down on— where did I see that? [Eight minutes on possible dining establishments to visit.]